THIS CHRISTMAS

THIS CHRISTMAS

Seasonal Poems for Peace

TERRY-LYNN JOHNSON

Waterside Productions

Copyright © 2024 by Terry-Lynn Johnson

www.lakeheadpoet.com

All rights reserved. This book or any portion thereof may not be reproduced or used in any manner whatsoever without the express written permission of the publisher except for the use of brief quotations in articles and book reviews.

NO AI TRAINING: Without in any way limiting the author's [and publisher's] exclusive rights under copyright, any use of this publication to "train" generative artificial intelligence (AI) technologies to generate text is expressly prohibited. The author reserves all rights to license uses of this work for generative AI training and development of machine learning language models.

First Printing, 2024

ISBN-13: 978-1-962984-32-4 paperback edition
ISBN-13: 978-1-962984-33-1 e-book edition

Waterside Productions
2055 Oxford Ave
Cardiff, CA 92007
www.waterside.com

DEDICATION

*To my Guardian Aunt and Uncle
George and Ellen Nicholl*

Christmas just isn't Christmas without you.

Table of Contents

Foreword..ix
Acknowledgement..xi
Introduction..xiii

A Christmas Prayer..1
The Red Mailbox...2
The Donkey..3
Red Cardinal..4
Christmas Wish..5
Hard Candy Christmas......................................6
Snow Globe..7
Sprigs of Holly...8
Old Downtown Christmas....................................9
Forecast of Snow...10
Morning Flurries...11
Grey Jay...12
Black Capped Chickadee...................................13
Festival of Lights.......................................14
Season of Old..15
Candlelight Service......................................17
Olive Wood Cross...18
Christmas Garland..19
Season Snowfall..20
Woodland Cabin...21

Winter Jay 22
Old Father Time 23
Winter Starlight 24
Winter Carols 25
Winter Grace 26

Index of Opening Phrases 29
About the Author. 31
Index of Re-Published Poems. 33

Foreword

I was introduced to Canadian Poet Terry-Lynn Johnson through my dear friend William Gladstone of Waterside Productions with publication of *Driftwood Tones: Nature Poetry of Beauty & Presence* (2023).

Since our introduction, our friend William (Bill) Gladstone made his transition to the other side. His life was a life dedicated to supporting authors as they step into greatness by getting their books of truth, courage and wisdom into the world. He inspired greatness in us all, need I say more...

For those of you who are just getting to know Terry-Lynn, she has gone through many challenges and has put her pain, passion, joy, love and wisdom into her poetry. Her poetry is deep, real, and causes the reader to stop, slow down and contemplate what is common to human experience.

Terry-Lynn is a master of the art of presence. She has a unique ability to awaken the inner child, soul wisdom, and brilliance which lies within us. She crafts her lyrics with beauty and peace which synchronizes with your intimate presence. She shares with you her own faith and hope through the joy of celebrating the birth of Christ and Christmas traditions. This new publication *This Christmas: Seasonal Poems for Peace* with Waterside Productions inspires a culture of peace and goodwill which is the basis of wisdom and enlightenment.

The publication is exceptional and timely. There may always be cycles of uncertainty, fears of economic disasters, wars, poverty, and lack, but I can assure you if you connect deeply to Terry Lynn's poetry you will find solace, peace, and the promises of the Master of Christmas.

The poetry in *This Christmas* raises consciousness with the joy and peace of the season. The poem "Season of Old" brings you to the magic of Christmas as points of constellations sparkle in the clear night sky. The joy of the season is caught in the simple lyrics of "Black Capped Chickadee" with pure notes of greeting. The simple faith of the season is found in "Olive Wood Cross" with the choir caroling Christmas hymns of peace.

One of my personal favorites "Winter Grace" concludes with "all is well with my soul" in the setting of a frosted morning with sullen notes of the songbird. I encourage you to dwell on what it means for you to realize that all is well with your soul.

The publication of *This Christmas: Seasonal Poems for Peace* with its twenty-five poems is a hallmark. The brevity and beauty of the lyrics enhances the descriptive verse as you imagine the beauty and peace of natural settings with winter scenery. I as you will treasure this collection of seasonal poetry for many Christmases to come.

Many Blessings...

Live life with Courage,

Ken D. Foster
Voices of Courage.us
KenDFoster.com

Acknowledgement

Family & Friends

Thank you to my husband for being there for me through the thick and thin with devoted love. And to my son and daughter for their on-going support. You both mean so much to me. I am grateful for my two delightful grandchildren who fill my heart with joy. And I am grateful for my extended family and friends. Although life gets too busy at times to get together, I appreciate your love and support. To my loved ones who have passed on and are often close in my thoughts. And above all, thank you to Christ my Saviour for walking with me and giving me both strength and guidance.

Introduction

Let there be peace on earth
Peace be with you this Christmas

A Christmas Prayer

The season of peace
is drawing nigh
As a dusting of snow
lays out the bedding
for late frost.
The pigeons roost
on the gables of
the old inn
And my soul petitions
for peace with
the silent night.

The Red Mailbox

There is a
Christmas card
in the red mailbox
posted to you
Capped with an
angel's dusting
of snow
and holly.

The Donkey

The small donkey
that carried Mary
with child
into Bethlehem
knew the weight
of his burden.
You too, my child,
know the weight
of burden with
His plans for
you.
Be blessed.

RED CARDINAL

Post me a card of
the red Christmas bird
with holly
As the cardinal
does not venture here.
And I will post
a northern winter scene
to you.
Maybe next year
I will visit
With the cardinal's
whistle over the
season.

CHRISTMAS WISH

The Star of Bethlehem
shines over the nativity
manger scene
As we celebrate our
Christmas traditions.
What is this day?
O' Prince of Peace.
Let us pray
For peace on earth
this Christmas.

Hard Candy Christmas

Christmas socks
are hung by the tree
with peppermint
candy
And gifts are placed
from Santa's Cheer
As children dream of reindeer
hooves in the starlit sky.
It's a hard candy
Christmas
this year.

Snow Globe

Your calico cat
curls on the mat
in front of the warmth
of the fireplace
And dreams
of the magical world
of the snow globe
on the mantel.

Sprigs of Holly

Snow brings nostalgia
for season past—
With street lamps aglow
And snowflakes blanketing
the parkway path.
French pane windows
with decorative wreaths
Carollers with sheet notes
of goodwill and peace.
And baskets with sprigs
of holly.

Old Downtown Christmas

Victorian carollers
bring seasonal charm
to Christmas window
displays
Shoppers rush
and handbells ring
for Christmas Cheer
Sweethearts at the skating park
share hopes for the new year
And snow flurries bring
the magic of season
to the downtown
core.

Forecast of Snow

Snowflakes reflect in
pewter skies with dawn
As I let my dog out
to frolic in the yard.
And curl up with a book
to read.
The snow softly blankets
the quiet hours
And snow angels
imprint with forecast
of joy and magical
peace.

Morning Flurries

The sweet notes of songbirds
rise from shelter of branch
As the wintry morning breaks
with peace.
The beauty of flurries blanketed
with bedding of soft light—
Under slate morning greys
with winter skies.

GREY JAY

The grey jay with ruffled coat
lands on the tailgate
As he brazenly forages
for scraps.
The camp setting
spruce backwoods with
December rain.
The friendly jay good company
on the northern winter trail.

Black Capped Chickadee

The black capped
chickadees
string pure notes
of greeting
from the snow ladened
boughs of cedar.
I must get out
in crisp and cold air
to find joy in the day
As you, robust little
chickadee.

Festival of Lights

The air is crisp
with winter evening
As you enjoy the lakefront
festival of lights
Your dog intent on scent
of reindeer footprints afield.
The crystal snow over the lake
reflects the Christmas Star
And children's faces
delight with the festival
of lights
Under woolly toques.

SEASON OF OLD

The night is bright with stars above,
and the soft blanket of snow
reflects hope.
Goodwill is packaged fruit cake.
And handbells resonate
singular notes
of old faith.

Candles are cupped by carolers
with hope,
as flurries blanket frozen hills.
Children are bundled
with bright scarves.
Pulling sleds
and lacing skates.

The snow falls lightly
as the evening wears on.
And children's cheeks are rosy,
as they cozy under plaid throws
with mitts wrapped around
steaming mugs.

Children are tucked in for the night
with promise of reindeer
prancing on roofs.
And with cookies left out on plates.
The points of constellations
sparkle in the night sky
which is now clear.

Pause is given to the year past
with snow drifts on front steps.
Greeting cards refrain peace on earth
and goodwill.
Mitts with strings are hung to dry
like musical notes on lines
under the night sky.

Candlelight Service

The new year promises
precious moments
As I take your frail hand
And you worry about
plans for the season.
You wrap your scarf
over your top coat
The white pine branches
weighted with snow.
Handbells ring in crystal air
with starlit skies.
Homeward bound
Bearing candles into
the night.

Olive Wood Cross

We head out for
the evening
to enjoy the choir
Mom with frail health
And simple faith.
The olive wood cross
on the altar.
The choir carols
White Christmas
And news of war
rounds into the
new year.
The heavenly hymn
of Silent Night
bringing peace to
the evening.

CHRISTMAS GARLAND

String moments
with garland beads
around the tree
this Christmas.
And be blessed
with simpler joys
this year.

Season Snowfall

The evening is bright
with light snow falling at dusk—
blanketing our world with delight.
Shall we venture out together
into winter hinterland—
And enjoy a camper's mug
of hot chocolate?
Or just gaze out at the beauty of
the evening's snow
And snuggle under a cabin fleece throw
As we reflect on our plans
for the holidays.

Woodland Cabin

The poet retreats to the
warmth of the log cabin
And smoke wafts from the
stone fireplace into winter sky.
The whitetail doe and fawn
stand still in pine—
With snowflakes falling quietly
over the woodland.
The poet sits to write by
the sash window of the cabin
Posting an idyllic scene
of greeting to you.

Winter Jay

Silent snowflakes
fall with angelic
rise and lift
As the jay darts to
snow-capped branch
with scent of pine.
The awakening peace
of early hours reflected
in morning light.

Old Father Time

There is a lull in the season
before the new year
With a feeling of content
of time well spent with family
and friends—
You sit by the fireplace
and marvel
at old Father Time.
How yet another season passes
into a new calendar year—
And at how, as time passes,
blessings are the simpler
things in life.

Winter Starlight

Wintering birds
shelter with stillness
under mystic starlight
And you settle to rest
Knowing what it is
to walk, and weep
with Christ.

Winter Carols

The ice crystal snow
reflects the stillness
of morning
The chimney smoke
from the warm cabin
flattened with ceiling
of cold
The winter songbird
settles with daybreak
of a clear winter sky
And carols notes
of Hallelujah—
Christ is born
this day.

Winter Grace

Sullen notes
uplift in frosted
branches
Reflecting
morning light
with comfort of
midwinter
song.
All is well with
my soul.

Index of Opening Phrases

Christmas socks are hung by the tree with peppermint candy (6)
Post me a card of the red Christmas bird with holly (4)
Silent snowflakes fall with angelic rise and lift (22)
Snow brings nostalgia for season past (8)
Snowflakes reflect in pewter skies with dawn (10)
String moments with garland beads around the tree (19)
Sullen notes uplift in frosted branches (26)
The air is crisp with winter evening (14)
The black capped chickadees string pure notes of greeting (13)
The evening is bright with light snow falling at dusk (20)
The grey jay with ruffled coat lands on the tailgate (12)
The ice crystal snow reflects the stillness of morning (25)
The new year promises precious moments (17)
The night is bright with stars above (15)
The poet retreats to the warmth of the log cabin (21)
The season of peace is drawing nigh (1)
The small donkey that carried Mary with child (3)
The Star of Bethlehem shines over the
nativity manger scene (5)
The sweet notes of songbirds rise from shelter of branch (11)
There is a Christmas card in the red mailbox (2)
There is a lull in the season before the new year (23)
We head out for the evening to enjoy the choir (18)

Wintering birds shelter with stillness (24)
Victorian carollers bring seasonal charm
to Christmas window displays (9)
Your calico cat curls on the mat (7)

About the Author

Terry-Lynn Johnson is a modern romantic poet. Her poetry includes themes of nature, beauty and spirituality. She was born in Nipigon, Ontario and is a graduate of Lakehead University. She attained a Master of Education with undergraduate degrees of Honours Bachelor of Arts and Bachelor of Education.

Previous publications of poetry include *"Sprigs and Twigs: A Solitary Note & Selected Poems (Collector's Edition)* (FriesenPress, 2021) and *"Driftwood Tones: Nature Poetry of Beauty & Presence"* (Waterside Productions, 2023).

Her favourite poets include Leonard Cohen, Maya Angelou and Robert Frost with an interest in Romantic, Victorian and modern poetry. She enjoys the contemporary poetry of Atticus and the nature poetry of Wendell Berry and Mary Oliver. She started writing poetry at the age of twelve.

She lives on the scenic northwestern shores of Lake Superior and enjoys the outdoors, walks with her dog and time with her family. Her husband is a professional musician. They perform acoustic music and poetry at a variety of venues.

Index of Re-Published Poems

from *Driftwood Tones: Nature Poetry of Beauty & Presence*
Waterside Productions, 2023

The Red Mailbox
The Donkey
Snow Globe
Sprigs of Holly
Forecast of Snow
Black Capped Chickadee
Season of Old
Candlelight Service
Season Snowfall
Old Father Time

www.ingramcontent.com/pod-product-compliance
Lightning Source LLC
Chambersburg PA
CBHW071953070426
42451CB00015BA/3449